For Cheryl Vance,
A Fellow Book - and Lizard - Lover!

Sneed B. Collard III!!!
2012

SNEED B. COLLARD III'S MOST FUN BOOK EVER ABOUT

LIZARDS

Charlesbridge

To Roman Geoffrey Dawson

Published by Charlesbridge
85 Main Street
Watertown, MA 02472
(617) 926-0329
www.charlesbridge.com

Library of Congress Cataloging-in-Publication Data
Collard, Sneed B.
Sneed B. Collard III's most fun book ever about lizards / Sneed B. Collard III.
    p. cm.
    ISBN 978-1-58089-324-4 (reinforced for library use)
    ISBN 978-1-58089-325-1 (softcover)
1. Lizards—Miscellanea. 2. Lizards as pets. I. Title.
QL666.L2C58 2012
597.95—dc22
                                                2011000809

Display type set in Animated Gothic and
    text type set in Adobe Caslon
Color separations by KHL Chroma Graphics, Singapore
Printed and bound September 2011 by Imago in Singapore
Production supervision by Brian G. Walker
Designed by Susan Mallory Sherman

Printed in Singapore
(hc)   10 9 8 7 6 5 4 3 2 1
(sc)   10 9 8 7 6 5 4 3 2 1

All photographs courtesy of Sneed B. Collard III, with the exception of the following:
© Jack Grove, JSGrove Photography www.jsgrove.com, pp. 1, 6, 11, 21, 37 (bottom), 45
© McDonald Wildlife Photography, Inc., pp. 15, 29, 37 (top), 48

A Bowl of Flies, I mean, Thanks!

The author (me) would like to extend a chameleonlike tongue of thanks to the following lizard lovers who helped me learn about and photograph many of the saurians in this book:

❋ Jessi Knudsen Castañeda and Augusto Castañeda of Animal Wonders Inc., a great educational group that shares its love of lizards and other animals with kids of all ages

❋ The fun folks (and lizards) at Pet Nebula—the coolest pet store in Montana

❋ McDonald Wildlife Photography, Inc.

❋ Jack Grove, excellent photographer, guide, and friend

❋ The Phoenix Zoo

❋ Mark A. Johnson

I'd also like to extend a special thanks to my editor, Randi Rivers, who once again persevered through the sun, rain, and snow to see this book to completion!

---

cover: green iguana

back cover: baby chameleon

page 1: friends to the tail end

title page: A western skink's dazzling and detachable decoy in case a hungry bird spies this lizard from overhead.

above: eyelash, or crested, gecko

Table of Contents

crocodile monitor lizard

So Many Lizards, So Little Information

Most people don't know very much about lizards. This seems odd when you consider that lizards—or saurians, as they are sometimes called—are the most common reptiles on the planet. According to the German Herpetological Society's TIGR Reptile Database (www.reptile-database.org), scientists have described more than five thousand species of lizards—more than all other reptiles combined.

So why don't people know much about lizards? Maybe we don't bother learning about them because lizards can't win football games or help us with our homework. Maybe lizards are so common we simply overlook them. But maybe, just maybe, we don't know about lizards because most of us have never had the chance to. . . .

opposite: Galapagos marine iguanas gather in large numbers to soak up some rays and conserve heat between feeding forays into the chilly ocean.

Meet Joe Lizard

Your average "Joe Lizard" is a western fence lizard, but his fans call him "blue belly." He's about three and a half inches (nine centimeters) long—not counting that handsome tail—and is about as typical a lizard as you can get.

Let's start with that scaly skin. Those scales make Joe look kinda cool, but they are mighty useful as well. They're made from keratin—the same stuff as your fingernails—and are tough enough to keep Joe from getting cut or scratched. They also help prevent Joe's body from losing moisture. This comes

California's best-known saurian, the western fence lizard, isn't just another pretty face; it has super survival traits, including the ability to live in many habitats.

in handy seeing as how lizards live in some of the world's driest places, including Joe's home in Southern California. Joe's scaly skin blends in well with his surroundings. Camouflage is extremely popular in the lizard world. It helps lizards hide from enemies and sneak up on prey. Flip Joe Lizard over, though, and you'll discover why his fans call him blue belly. Isn't that the prettiest rib cage you've ever seen? Herpetologists—people who study reptiles and amphibians—think Joe Lizard flashes his bright blue colors to attract mates and warn intruders to stay out of his territory.

Speaking of territories, Joe's territory is where he hunts and goes a-courtin' for female lizards. Joe also spends a lot of time there basking, or lying around, in the sun. Don't call him "Lazy Joe," though. Joe is an ectotherm—an animal that can't make its own heat. He has to bask to raise his body temperature.

A western fence lizard's bright blue "siding" helps males attract mates while warning other males to "get lost."

Measuring a Lizard

Scientists often don't include the tail when measuring a lizard's length. Instead, they measure only from the animal's snout to its anus, or vent. This is called the snout-vent length. Why do scientists leave off the tail length? One good reason is that lizards often lose their tails. Because of this, a tail length can give a false impression of how large the animal actually is. Tails also naturally come in many lengths, from long to short. They just aren't useful indicators of how old or big or healthy an animal might be.

Like most lizards, Joe eats just about anything he can stuff down his gullet: insects, spiders, scorpions, centipedes—sometimes even other lizards. Of course, he's on the menu, too, so he has to watch his scaly back. Snakes, cats, roadrunners, and other predators are always on the prowl for a lizard lunch. If Joe Lizard falls into the clutches of an enemy, he may resort to one of his coolest tricks—dropping his tail. With luck, this startles the predator and allows Joe to make a getaway. What about the tail? Joe will miss it, but he'll soon get busy growing a new one.

If you think Joe's cool, just wait till you meet some of the . . . .

Stars of the Lizard World

Like Joe, most lizards aren't famous. You won't see them on talk shows or splashed across newspaper headlines. But if Hollywood had a Walk of Fame for lizards (and I, for one, think it should), here are a few saurians you'd be sure to find there.

Komodo Dragons or Oras

Komodo dragons are not actual dragons. They belong to a group of about fifty lizards called monitor lizards. All monitors are large as lizards go, but the Komodo dragon, or *ora*, is the size champ. It grows up to 10 feet (3 meters) long and can weigh more than 300 pounds (136 kilograms)! Other monitor lizards may grow a bit longer (thanks to their tails), but no other lizard competes for the *ora's* heavyweight title.

Oras live only on six small islands in Indonesia, including the island of Komodo. Little Komodo dragons catch insects such as grasshoppers to eat. Adults scavenge for food or chase down goats, cattle, and even an occasional tourist trying to take a picture. This makes them the only living lizards known to eat people.

Territories Big and Small

It's no surprise that the size of a lizard's territory depends on the size of the lizard. For small lizards, such as Joe Lizard, a territory might be smaller than a person's bedroom. For large lizards, such as the Komodo dragon, it could spread over several square miles. Territory size also depends on how much food is available. The less food, the larger a lizard's territory needs to be.

opposite: The Komodo dragon is not only the world's largest lizard, but it's also the only one known to eat people. That guy with the stick had best watch out!

Gila Monsters

Just as Komodo dragons are not actual dragons, Gila monsters are not actual monsters. You will never see them in a movie called *Alien vs. Gila Monster*. They are, however, one of only two or three lizards in the world that are known to be venomous. The others are Mexican beaded lizards and, scientists now believe, Komodo dragons.

Gila monsters live in the deserts of the American Southwest. They spend most of their time in underground burrows that they dig with their sharp claws. This allows them to avoid extremely hot and cold temperatures—and to keep the glare off their television screens while they watch reruns of *Saurian Idol*.

Gila monsters move slowly, but what's the hurry? They eat things such as baby birds, bird eggs, and other prey that can't get away. They also have little to fear from other animals. Their bright orange and black colors warn, "I'm venomous. Don't mess with me." While their venom won't send a person to the grave, it can give a careless cowboy a painful reminder to keep his distance.

Sunburn? No. But a Gila monster's bright warning colors don't just deter predators—they may also help you keep from stepping on the Gila monster on the way to the school bus.

"Yeah, I'm lookin' at you—and you, too!" This baby chameleon has its eyes peeled for danger. A chameleon's independent eyes can stare down two objects at once.

Chameleons

One writer calls chameleons "the most perfectly adapted lizards ever." At the recent World's Most Evolved Reptile Championships on Lizard Island, Australia, chameleons won trophies for

❀ the ability to change color to match their surroundings

❀ eyes that can move independently of each other

❀ tails that can grab onto branches and twigs

❀ ridiculously long, lightning-fast tongues that can shoot out the length of the chameleons' bodies and can be fired at insects and other prey

Okay, I admit it. There isn't really a Most Evolved Reptile Championships. If there *were*, however, chameleons would also win a special jury prize for having horns, crowns, and other ornaments that put the best-dressed Hollywood actors to shame!

Chameleons generally live in trees, but they are experts at "dropping out of sight." If a predator tries to sneak up on one, the chameleon simply lets go of the branch it's sitting on. After falling twenty to thirty feet, the chameleon grabs another branch, safe again in its green forest mansion.

Note to insects: Put a lot of space between you and a panther chameleon, unless you want to become lunch—that tongue has range!

15

Thanks to their camouflage, armor plating, and large size, common iguanas thrive in the lizard-eat-lizard world of tropical forests.

Iguanas

You think you have a lot of relatives? Try dropping in on an iguana family reunion. There are about eight hundred species of lizards in the iguana family. The best known are the large common, or green, iguanas that live in the forests of Central and South America. Common iguanas grow as long as six feet (two meters). Flies and beetles? Don't insult their taste buds! These iguanas are vegetarians, eating leaves, fruit, flowers, and other plant material.

Like Joe Lizard, common iguanas can be pretty macho. They defend their territories and warn other lizards to stay away by lifting their bodies and bobbing their heads. Common iguanas spend most of their time in trees but descend to feed on plants on the forest floor. These large, leaf-eating lizards can be tamed and make popular pets—at least when they're small. Iguana owners often wish they'd bought a Chihuahua when their iguanas grow to full size and begin . . .

opposite: Ready for rugby? Well, maybe not, but when helmeted iguanas aren't chillin' in trees, they will take on a scrum of butterfly and beetle larvae.

What Do You Call a Bunch of Lizards?

If a group of kangaroos is called a "mob," and a group of whales is a "pod," what do we call a group of lizards?

One popular answer is a "lounge" of lizards. However, I believe that lizards are highly insulted by this term. While it's true that lizards do lounge around, they also work hard catching insects, chasing off intruders, and making more lizards. So what would a better word be?

I, Sneed B. Collard III, the author of this book—and friend of Joe Lizard—would, right now, like to propose that a group of lizards henceforth and forever be called a *scamper*.

What do you think? Can you think of something better? If so, I'd like to hear it. Send your answers to Sneed B. Collard III, P.O. Box 8507, Missoula, Montana 59807.

For a juvenile bearded dragon, there's always room in the gullet for one more cricket.

Eating Like a Lizard

Lizards have some of the most robust appetites of any reptiles. This isn't surprising, since lizards usually have a lot more zip than their turtle, snake, and crocodilian cousins.

The lizard menu stretches longer than an unraveled roll of toilet paper. Some lizards, such as the bearded dragon, are omnivores. They dine on a wide variety of plant and animal dishes. Other lizards, such as the common iguana, are vegetarians and eat mainly leaves, flowers, and fruit. However, Joe Lizard and most other lizard species stick to a lively diet. Anoles, for instance, provide top-notch pest-control services by devouring insects. Other lizards eat birds, rodents, worms, deer, other reptiles—almost anything that runs, crawls, flies, or breathes.

A long, forked tongue allows monitor lizards to pick up odors from more than 2 miles away.

Making Lizard Sense

A lizard's senses are extremely important in helping it obtain food. Many lizards have excellent eyesight and a keen sense of smell. Lizards smell through their noses, but they also have the help of Jacobson's organs, located in the roofs of their mouths. When a lizard sticks out its tongue, scent particles cling to it. When the tongue is withdrawn, these scent particles are transferred to the Jacobson's organ, giving the lizard information about possible food sources and dangers in the surrounding area.

It may seem stranger than fiction, but many lizards have a "third eye," called a pineal eye, on top of their heads. The pineal eye is covered by a layer of skin and is not as fully developed as the other two eyes. Scientists believe that this third eye probably helps a lizard determine day length. This, in turn, may affect the lizard's schedule for basking, feeding, hibernating, and breeding.

Lizards have a variety of ways of grabbing a meal. Many use a "sit and wait" strategy. Australian thorny devils and American horned lizards (aka horny toads) simply park next to ant trails and begin snatching up ants. In a single sitting, a thorny devil has been known to chow down twenty-five hundred ants—*without dipping sauce!*

A lot of other lizards hunt down their meals. Monitor lizards have powerful front legs, which they use to dig up eggs from crocodile nests.

In general, lizards aren't big water sports enthusiasts, but some—including Chinese crocodile lizards and several kinds of monitors—inhabit fresh and salt waters. They dive underwater in search of fish, crustaceans, and other aquatic animals.

Geckos have special gripping pads on their toes that allow them to pursue cockroaches, beetles, and moths on tree trunks and other vertical surfaces. A porch light surrounded by moths is a gecko's version of a fast food restaurant!

Two iguanas from the Galapagos Islands have come up with daring dining solutions. The land iguana eats cactuses—spines and all—by grinding up spiny mouthfuls with its armor-plated palate. The marine iguana makes an even bigger dining splash. It is the only marine lizard—one that spends much of its time in the ocean. When it's hungry, it dives underwater to graze on marine algae.

Of course, finding food isn't everything to a lizard. Just as important is . . .

"Want to grab a bite?" Grabbing is easy for many geckos, even for this shy guy, thanks to the special pads that allow them to scale almost any surface.

opposite: Galapagos land iguanas obtain food and water from the prickly pear cactuses they eat. They use any leftover cactus spines as toothpicks—but only if their electric toothbrushes aren't working.

Staying Off the Menu

While lizards are avid hunters, they are also avidly *hunted*. Birds especially seem to have a taste for lizards. Roadrunners, kookaburras, motmots, and falcons all devour large numbers of saurians. Other lizard predators include snakes, monkeys, bigger lizards, and—for some lizard species—people.

When confronted, most lizards won't hesitate to try to bluff their way out of bad situations. Alligator lizards hiss loudly when disturbed. Others, such as bearded dragons, puff themselves up or raise spines, crests, or other parts of their bodies to make themselves appear "badder" than they really are. Australian blue-tongued skinks open their mouths wide and stick out their bright blue tongues. This serves as a warning—or perhaps insults the predators so that they go away!

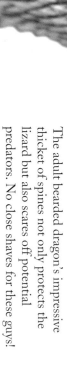

The adult bearded dragon's impressive thicket of spines not only protects the lizard but also scares off potential predators. No close shaves for these guys!

Effective camouflage? You bet. I ate my entire lunch within 15 feet of this large common basilisk before realizing it was lounging nearby.

How Long Do Lizards Live?

Scientists know very little about the life spans of most species, but for many lizards the best answer is "until they get eaten." Mortality for young lizards is extremely high. If they avoid ending up in someone else's stomach, most lizards can live for five to ten years. Gila monsters and Komodo dragons live around thirty years. According to one source, the world's longest-living lizards are a legless species called a slow worm. One of these critters lived for forty-seven years in the Copenhagen Zoo—almost long enough to collect Social Security benefits.

Lizards have a whole bag full of other tricks to stay off the menu. Common basilisks remain motionless most of the time. That, coupled with their superb camouflage, makes them almost impossible to detect among the leaves in their forest homes.

Horned lizards are also masters at camouflage, but they sometimes have to resort to Plan B. If a horned lizard is discovered, its formidable spines and armored plates make it difficult to attack and swallow. If all that fails, three species of horned lizards have evolved an additional gruesome defense. When captured or harassed, they squirt blood from their eyes. This blood may contain toxins, or it may just disgust the attacker enough to drop the lizard. Either way, the horned lizard is left free to go about its business.

Many lizards will drop tail and run to escape an enemy. Looking at the break line between old and new growth, it's obvious that this western fence lizard has lived to, *ahem*, tell the tale.

One of the most popular lizard defenses is a trick used by our friend Joe Lizard. Fence lizards, geckos, skinks, and many other lizards escape predators by dropping their tails. The tails have "break plates" built into their bones and tissues. Special muscles act like built-in tourniquets to keep the lizards from bleeding to death once the tail is dropped. Of course, it takes a lot of energy to grow a new tail, but many lizards get a head start by going back and eating their dropped appendages!

24

When push comes to shove, lizards can aggressively defend themselves. Monitor lizards are armed with sharp teeth and can slash away at enemies with their long tails. Gila monsters won't hesitate to clamp down on an attacker's nose or other appendage. People who've been bitten have needed to have the Gila monsters pried off with pliers or screwdrivers. Many lizards may take a nip at a predator, especially if they are "warmed up." And that brings us to a hot topic of saurian conversation . . .

As this Colombian black and white teiid lizard demonstrates, an open mouth—or "gape"—can help a saurian either cool down its body temperature or warn off an intruder. P-p-perhaps we should heed his warning and turn the page.

Lizards Hot and Cold

If you were a lizard—and who wouldn't want *that*—you wouldn't want to wake up in the morning thinking about French toast and orange juice. You'd be thinking about heat.

Like all animals, lizards need body heat to hunt, defend themselves, digest their food, reproduce, and play tennis. The ideal body temperature for most lizards seems to run between 95°F and 102°F (35°C and 39°C). But here's the problem: lizards are ectotherms—like Joe Lizard, they can't make their own body heat. All lizards have to get their heat from the surrounding environment. How do they deal with the body heat challenge? In one of two ways:

Some lizards are thermal conformers. They absorb heat from the air and soil and can function at a wide range of body temperatures. Geckos, for instance, perform better in warmer temperatures, but they are active mostly during cooler nighttime hours. This is when more prey and fewer predators are about. To handle their cooler lifestyle, geckos have adapted to stay active with body temperatures as low as 80°F (27°C).

Most other lizards, however, are thermal regulators. Unlike thermal conformers, thermal regulators must keep their bodies within a narrower, usually higher temperature range to stay active. Since they can't make their own heat, they rely on the greatest heating system ever invented—the sun.

Geckos such as this skunk, or white-lined, gecko are thermal conformers. Their bodies can function within a fairly wide range of temperatures. And, no, they don't spray predators—they get their name from the markings on their tail.

Thermal regulators have a fair share of adaptations that help them soak up the sun's rays. Horned lizards tilt their bodies so that more sun hits them. Other lizards darken their colors to absorb more heat. They do this by automatically changing the shapes of special skin cells that contain color pigments. The blood vessels of these lizards are especially good at quickly moving heat from the skin to other parts of the body that need it.

One iguanid lizard, *Liolaemus multiformis*, takes solar power to the extreme. These lizards live in the Peruvian Andes where temperatures often stay below freezing, even in full sunlight. After basking in the sun for only one hour, though, one iguanid's super-absorbent skin helped raise its temperature to 91°F (33°C)—56 degrees (31°C) warmer than the surrounding air temperature.

Of course lizards can get too hot as well as too cold. Most lizards will die if their bodies get warmer than 104°F (40°C). To keep from boiling over, desert lizards, such as Australia's thorny devil, move into the shade or retreat to underground burrows. Many desert lizards also have light skin that reflects the sun's rays, keeping the lizards cooler.

One final "hot tip": if you are a real lizard fan, you may have noticed that most large lizards live in warmer, tropical areas near the equator. Does this have anything to do with temperature? You bet your scales it does! Large lizards take longer to warm up in the sun than small lizards. In Canada or Chile, or even in Virginia, it would be almost impossible for a large lizard to ever soak up enough sun to get its motor running. That's why you never see large lizards taking ski vacations in Colorado or Utah. Only one lizard species—the European common lizard—survives above the Arctic Circle. Even in such a chilly environment, this lizard species makes time for . . .

¿Haga los lagartos hablan español? or, Do Lizards Speak Spanish?

Okay, they don't. But many of them *should*. Why? Being ectotherms, more lizard species live in the warm tropics than in temperate zones. Spanish-speaking countries such as Mexico, Colombia, and Panama abound with lizard species.

Parts of Asia, Africa, and Australia also have an abundance of saurians. As you move north and south from the equator, however, the number of lizard species declines dramatically. So beware of travel agencies that try to sell you lizard-watching holidays to Canada, Norway, or Siberia!

Believe it or not, this Texas horned lizard is not trying to display his best side to the camera. Like many desert-dwelling lizards, he's positioning himself for maximum sun exposure.

Falling in Love

Okay, lizards don't actually fall in love—not like we do, anyway. But making babies is a lizard's chief purpose in life, just as it is for every other animal. The first step is finding a mate.

Female lizards usually do the choosing in the mating game. During courtship, males put themselves on display. They drive fancy cars or flash wads of cash. Sometimes they wear gold jewelry.

Just kidding.

Lizards do know how to show off, though. Usually, males climb on rocks or tree trunks in the middle of their territories. Some display bright colors to females to say, "Hey, come and get me, baby!" Other male lizards show off fancy crests on their heads and backs. Anoles are famous for flaunting snazzy red or orange dewlaps beneath their throats. Males gain extra attention by bobbing their heads up and down and doing push-ups. All of these displays not only demonstrate a male's readiness to mate but also warn other males to keep to their own stomping grounds.

Of course bright colors and showy displays don't help nocturnal lizards—geckos and other saurians that are active at night. Males of nocturnal species rely on chirping sounds to attract females and to stake out their territories.

Whether he's nocturnal or not, a male lizard often mates with several females in his territory. Most lizards breed only during a specific season, usually when the weather is fine and food abounds. In the warm tropics, though, courtship and mating may take place throughout the year.

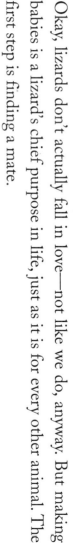

A dewlap under the chin is a snazzy way for males, like this green anole, to ask females, "Hey, baby, want to dance?"

opposite: True love? Well, probably not. Many male lizards mate with a number of different females.

One question I *know* you're asking yourself is, *Would I like to have lizards for my parents?* Trust me, the answer is a big fat NO! Most lizards make lousy parents. The female lays her eggs under a rock or in rotted wood or leaf litter. Then she takes off, leaving her eggs at the mercy of predators, weather, and chance. The number of eggs depends on the kind of lizard. Many geckos lay only one or two eggs. Horned lizards may lay more than twenty eggs.

Not all lizards lay eggs, of course. About one-fifth of lizard species give birth to live young—an adaptation to cooler climates. Just like adult lizards, baby lizards need warmth to grow and function. By carrying the young inside her, a mother lizard can find the warmest spots to bask in during the day and "incubate" her young inside her own body.

Want to hear something totally mind-blowing? Around thirty lizard species have gotten rid of mating altogether! This is called parthenogenesis (par-thuh-no-JEN-uh-sis), and it occurs naturally in a variety of animal groups. Take female whiptail lizards, for instance. Without mating or fertilization, some

Professional wrestling has nothing on this lizard takedown. Monitors and other lizards won't hesitate to defend their territories—and potential mates—against intruders and competitors.

32

Warm Fact

In some lizard species, the sex of the babies depends on the temperature at which the eggs develop. In the leopard gecko, eggs kept at 82°F (28°C) turn out to be mostly females. Eggs kept at 90°F (32°C) are mostly males.

Temperature also seems to affect the sex of some turtle and crocodilian offspring, but scientists still don't understand the significance of this process.

whiptail species lay eggs that produce female babies. These females, in turn, produce their own female offspring, again without mating.

Parthenogenesis gives lizards at least two advantages. One is that every lizard in a population can crank out more young and increase a population quickly. The other advantage is that a lizard moving to a new area—such as a resort in Hawaii or Palm Springs—doesn't need a mate to establish a new population there.

The disadvantage to parthenogenesis is that every lizard turns out to be identical to every other lizard in that population. None of the lizards have different features that could help them survive if the environment changed or if some disaster wiped out the rest of the population. Parthenogenetic lizard populations cannot evolve or adapt, and so they are more likely to become extinct. Unfortunately, in today's world, extinction is only one source of . . .

The western whiptail has given rise to another whiptail species that is comprised of all females. Astonishingly, these females do not need a mate to produce a healthy clutch of all-female babies!

33

Lizard Troubles

Like almost every other group of wild animals, lizards have suffered from the human conquest of planet Earth. Habitat destruction—the ruin of animal homes—is the biggest threat to most lizards. When humans burn or cut down forests, or bulldoze deserts to make cities, lizards can't just move into a new subdivision and start shopping at Reptile Mart. They have no way to survive.

Destruction of habitats—such as this former rain forest in Haiti—is the biggest threat to most lizard species.

Hunting is also a danger, especially for large lizards. After people settled on the island of Tonga about three thousand years ago, they quickly hunted the island's giant iguana species to extinction. Today, common iguanas are eaten in Central America and have disappeared from many regions. Each year people slaughter millions of monitor lizards and South American teiid lizards for their skins, which are turned into lizard-skin boots for wealthy Americans and Europeans. In many parts of the world, people kill lizards because they mistakenly believe the reptiles are venomous or because they look like snakes—a poor excuse to kill anything. Other threats to lizards include poisoning by pesticides, the destruction of grasslands by cattle, and collecting by pet traders.

Today many endangered lizards live on islands, where hunting, habitat destruction, and introduced predators—such as cats and rats—have greatly reduced their populations. National laws and international treaties protect some kinds of lizards. For instance, the government of Indonesia

34

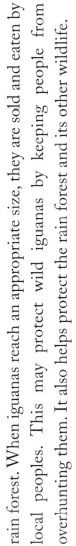

Millions of large teiid lizards are killed for their skins each year.

has protected the Komodo dragon. Komodos and several other lizards also receive protection from the Convention on International Trade of Endangered Species, or CITES. CITES is an agreement among many countries aimed at prohibiting the trade or sale of endangered animals and animal products. Unfortunately, not all countries enforce CITES, so illegal trade of lizards and other wild animals continues.

One unusual approach to protecting lizards is happening in Central America. Some people have started iguana farms, where these lizards are allowed to graze in protected areas of rain forest. When iguanas reach an appropriate size, they are sold and eaten by local peoples. This may protect wild iguanas by keeping people from overhunting them. It also helps protect the rain forest and its other wildlife.

But enough doom and gloom. Let's get back to the reason you picked up this book—lizards themselves! I can't think of a better way to do that than by looking at some of the world's greatest . . .

Lizard Olympians

There's one thing I learned early on while writing this book: every time you say something about lizards, some saurian comes along to make a liar out of you. Take locomotion or movement. Everybody knows that Joe and other lizards walk and run around on four legs, right? Well, not exactly.

Religious Lizards

When some lizards are in a hurry, there's no time for front legs. These species rise up on their hind limbs like sprinters at the NCAA Track and Field Championships. Bipedal (two-legged) locomotion allows them to run faster and outdistance predators. Basilisks, or Jesus Christ lizards, take it a step further. They can run on their hind legs *across water.* Fringed flaps on their toes fan out, keeping the basilisks from sinking. As you might guess, smaller basilisks zoom across water more easily than full-grown adults.

Basilisk lizards can race across the surface of streams and rivers; oh, and they're not too shabby at climbing trees either.

Leapin' Lizards

One problem with forests is that they don't have elevators or escalators. So both Draco lizards and flying geckos get around by gliding from tree to tree. How? They have evolved special skin flaps along their bodies and limbs that can be spread out to serve as wings. Flying geckos also have webbed feet that help them ride the sky. These skin flaps probably evolved as a camouflage aid, softening the edges of the geckos' bodies against their backgrounds. But you know the old saying: "Have flaps, will glide."

Dive Masters

Most lizards are landlubbers. As we've seen, however, some species lead wet-and-wild lifestyles. Most remarkable are the Galapagos marine iguanas. Their flattened, streamlined bodies and partially webbed feet allow them to dive to depths of almost one hundred feet (thirty meters) to obtain the seaweed that they eat. Galapagos waters are very cold, but diving iguanas conserve body heat by slowing their heart rate and keeping blood flow away from their skin.

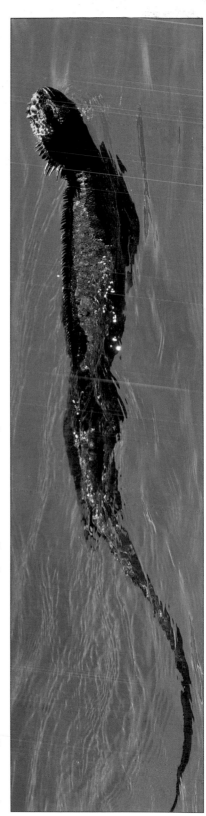

By spreading its rib cage, a Draco unfurls its flaps to fly.

The Galapagos marine iguana is the only lizard known to dive to great depths for food.

Saurian Subways

Here is a fascinating fact: not all lizards have four legs. Many have only two legs, while others have none! Lizards that are short on legs are usually fossorial. This means that they spend most of their time underground or under rotting logs and other objects. Glass lizards, blind lizards, and legless lizards all live fossorial lifestyles. These animals move by "swimming" through sand or across the ground. Living underground offers lizards many advantages. It allows them to avoid windblown sands and extreme temperatures. Just as important, it allows them to hunt termites and other underground prey. Important point: lizards without legs *are not snakes!* They are simply lizards that have evolved a "snaky" way of getting around.

If you need some extra lunch money, try betting one of your friends—or better yet, your parents—that this eastern glass lizard is a lizard, not a snake. Easy money!

Is It a Lizard or a Snake?

Snakes and lizards are very closely related, and it's not always easy to tell a legless lizard from a snake. One difference is that lizards have movable eyelids, while snakes don't. If you flip over a snake, you also may find that it has only one long row of scales on its belly. Lizards often have several rows of belly scales. Lizard skeletons also have a forward pelvic girdle bone, even if the lizards are legless. Snake skeletons have completely lost this forward set of hips through evolution.

38

Juvenile black ctenosaur lizards are not only a different color from their more drab parents, they are also much speedier. They have to be to avoid the many predators that would like to munch on them.

From the Record Books

The title for World's Fastest Lizard used to belong to the African race runner lizard. A person in a car clocked one of these supercharged critters tearing up the turf at 18 miles (29 kilometers) per hour! More recently, Guinness World Records listed a black ctenosaur's (TEE-no-sorz) sprint speed at 21.7 miles (34.6 kilometers) per hour. Hmm . . . is there a saurian showdown coming down the pike?

Lizards as Pets

You don't need to own a lizard to observe one. Many people have lizards living in their backyards or on their porches. To watch one, all you have to do is go outside, sit down, and keep your eyes open.

Still, more and more people keep saurians as pets. There are many reasons. Most lizards are small, so they don't take up much space. Many are friendly and easy to handle. Lizards are also much more interesting to watch than *SpongeBob SquarePants* and *iCarly*. With all these things going for them, shouldn't everyone have a pet lizard?

Absolutely not!

I believe that most people should not own lizards. Here are four reasons why:

✺ Each kind of lizard has its own special requirements necessary for survival and health. Yet 99 percent of pet owners don't take the time to find out what their lizards need. As a result, most captive lizards end up dying—a cruel fate for such wonderful creatures.

✺ Many popular lizards, such as iguanas and monitors, grow quite large. Pet owners freak out when their cute little iguanas grow into six-foot (two-meter) eating machines with fearsome claws and teeth.

✺ Lizards live for a long time. New lizard owners often love these animals but then grow tired of them. Unwanted lizards become *mistreated* lizards—another unfair fate.

Take me home! If you just have to have a lizard for a pet, a bearded dragon (like Whiskers here) is a good, captive-bred choice.

Love me! All pet lizards require dedicated care in order to stay healthy and happy.

42

✿ People who grow tired of their lizards often release them in places that are not the lizards' natural environments. These lizards either die or become problems for native animals and plants. For instance, Cuban anoles have driven out native anoles from Miami and surrounding areas.

If you're still determined to have a pet lizard, here are some suggestions:

❀ Catch a common, non-dangerous, local species and keep it in a terrarium with food and water for a few days. Then return it to the place you caught it. This will allow you to enjoy and learn about the animal without harming it.

❀ If you buy a pet lizard, make certain it has been captive bred, instead of being caught in the wild. This will ensure that you are not depleting populations of wild lizards. Ask your pet dealer for proof that your lizard was not captured in the wild.

❀ Always read as much as possible about your saurian so you know how to properly take care of it. All lizards need water, food, natural light, shade, and a slew of other things to stay healthy. Pet stores often provide this information. Lizard care books also are available for some lizard species. If there isn't one for your lizard, it probably isn't a species you should keep as a pet.

❀ NEVER EVER release a store-bought or exotic lizard (or any other animal) into the wild! This is cruel to the lizard and may end up hurting other animals in your area. Lizards are living, breathing creatures. If you buy a lizard, you must be committed to it for *its* entire life—not just until you get bored with it.

Captive-bred chameleons make interesting pets, but DO NOT try to move your eyes like they do, or you may be mistaken for a chameleon and be forced to eat grasshoppers and praying mantises.

Lizards—The Tail End

Well, are you as excited about lizards as I am? If not, we won't invite you to any lizard slumber parties—which are held on warm rocks in the middle of the day. Whether you're up for a slumber party or not, I hope that this book has whet your appetite for lizards and that you'll want to learn even more about them.

Unfortunately, most lizard-related websites focus on selling things, and there aren't nearly enough good lizard books available. That's why I wrote this one. If you're hungering for more, though, try gulping down these tasty reptile reads:

Brown, David E., and Neil B. Carmony. *Gila Monster: Facts and Folklore of America's Aztec Lizard*. Salt Lake City: University of Utah Press, 1999.

Darling, Kathy. *Komodo Dragons: On Location*. New York: Harper-Collins, 1997.

Mattison, Chris. *Lizards of the World*. New York: Facts On File, 2004.

Pianka, Eric R., and Laurie J. Vitt. *Lizards: Windows to the Evolution of Diversity*. Berkeley: University of California Press, 2003. (This adult book is not as funny as mine, but it's full of amazing facts.)

So what are you waiting for? Go watch some lizards for yourself and learn everything there is to know about them. Then sit back, munch on a few insects, and warm your belly on a hot rock. You'll realize—just like Joe Lizard does— that even a simple life can be pretty fine. Or, as Joe would say, "Fly fine."

A basking marine iguana makes a perfect perch for a lava lizard wanting to see the world!

45

Glossary

amphibians: cold-blooded animals that live in water and breathe using gills until they reach adulthood, when they develop lungs and live on land

basking: lying in a warm place, usually in the sun, to raise body temperature

bipedal locomotion: two-legged movement

camouflage: coloration or other type of disguise that allows an animal to blend in with its surroundings and go undetected by predators

crest: a tuft located at the top of an animal's head that is often used in courtship and defensive displays

dewlap: loose skin on a lizard's throat that can be extended for courtship or warning displays

ectotherm: an animal that can't make its own body heat

fossorial: spending time in burrows or underground

habitat destruction: the ruin of animal homes

herpetologist: a scientist who studies reptiles and amphibians

Jacobson's organ: a sensor in the roof of a lizard's mouth that captures chemical sensory information about the surrounding environment

keratin: a strong protein that helps form a lizard's scales

lizard: a reptile that usually has a long, scaly body

marine lizard: a saurian that spends much of its time in the ocean

monitor lizards: a group of large, meat-eating saurians

nocturnal: active at night

omnivore: an animal that eats both plant and animal material

parthenogenesis: spontaneous reproduction without fertilization

pineal eye: a "third eye" located on top of a lizard's head that scientists believe may help the lizard determine day length

plates: toughened skin that helps protect various parts of a lizard's body

predators: animals that hunt other animals as a source of food

reptiles: cold-blooded animals with a backbone that are usually covered in scales

saurians: another name for lizards

scale: a protective covering found on most reptiles that keeps their skin moist and safe from scratches

spine: a pointed, sharp growth on some animals that is used in courtship and defensive displays

territory: the area where an animal lives, hunts, and breeds

thermal conformers: animals that can function in a wide range of body temperatures and receive their heat from the surrounding air and soil

thermal regulators: animals that need to keep their bodies within a narrow, typically high temperature range to stay active, usually receiving heat from the sun

Index

page 48: *A panther chameleon enjoys a lively snack.*

47